hello beautiful badass

A daily, weekly, and monthly planner with empowering sweary sayings for each week. Prepare to laugh and be reminded that you are indeed a beautiful badass who's doing a fucking awesome job at juggling life!

NEW BEGINNINGS CAN BE
FUCKING MAGICAL

DECEMBER

12/30/19 to 01/05/20

○ 30. MONDAY

○ 31. TUESDAY

○ 1. WEDNESDAY

○ 2. THURSDAY

○ 3. FRIDAY

○ 4. SATURDAY / 5. SUNDAY

IMPORTANT AS FUCK

SHIT TO DO

Notes and Shit

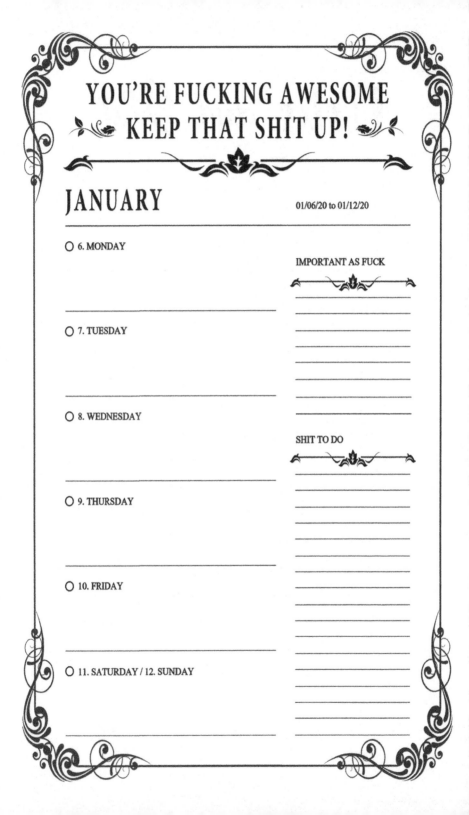

YOU'RE FUCKING AWESOME
KEEP THAT SHIT UP!

JANUARY

01/06/20 to 01/12/20

○ 6. MONDAY

IMPORTANT AS FUCK

○ 7. TUESDAY

○ 8. WEDNESDAY

SHIT TO DO

○ 9. THURSDAY

○ 10. FRIDAY

○ 11. SATURDAY / 12. SUNDAY

Notes and Shit

Make this week your bitch

JANUARY

01/13/20 to 01/19/20

○ 13. MONDAY

IMPORTANT AS FUCK

○ 14. TUESDAY

○ 15. WEDNESDAY

SHIT TO DO

○ 16. THURSDAY

○ 17. FRIDAY

○ 18. SATURDAY / 19. SUNDAY

Notes and Shit

Reminder: you do epic shit

JANUARY

01/20/20 to 01/26/20

○ 20. MONDAY

IMPORTANT AS FUCK

○ 21. TUESDAY

○ 22. WEDNESDAY

SHIT TO DO

○ 23. THURSDAY

○ 24. FRIDAY

○ 25. SATURDAY / 26. SUNDAY

Notes and Shit

Rise and fucking grind

JANUARY

01/27/20 to 02/02/20

O 27. MONDAY

IMPORTANT AS FUCK

O 28. TUESDAY

O 29. WEDNESDAY

SHIT TO DO

O 30. THURSDAY

O 31. FRIDAY

O 1. SATURDAY / 2. SUNDAY

Notes and Shit

Wake up. Kick ass. Repeat.

FEBRUARY

02/03/20 to 02/09/20

○ 3. MONDAY

IMPORTANT AS FUCK

○ 4. TUESDAY

○ 5. WEDNESDAY

SHIT TO DO

○ 6. THURSDAY

○ 7. FRIDAY

○ 8. SATURDAY / 9. SUNDAY

Notes and Shit

KEEP YOUR HEAD HIGH AND YOUR
MIDDLE FINGER HIGHER

FEBRUARY

02/10/20 to 02/16/20

O 10. MONDAY

IMPORTANT AS FUCK

O 11. TUESDAY

O 12. WEDNESDAY

SHIT TO DO

O 13. THURSDAY

O 14. FRIDAY

O 15. SATURDAY / 16. SUNDAY

Notes and Shit

Believe in your fucking self

FEBRUARY

02/17/20 to 02/23/20

O 17. MONDAY

O 18. TUESDAY

O 19. WEDNESDAY

O 20. THURSDAY

O 21. FRIDAY

O 22. SATURDAY / 23. SUNDAY

IMPORTANT AS FUCK

SHIT TO DO

Notes and Shit

REPLACE EVERY "WHAT IF" WITH "WHY THE FUCK NOT"

FEBRUARY

02/24/20 to 03/01/20

O 24. MONDAY

O 25. TUESDAY

O 26. WEDNESDAY

O 27. THURSDAY

O 28. FRIDAY

O 29. SATURDAY / 1. SUNDAY

IMPORTANT AS FUCK

SHIT TO DO

Notes and Shit

Bitch slap your stress away

MARCH

03/02/20 to 03/08/20

O 2. MONDAY

O 3. TUESDAY

O 4. WEDNESDAY

O 5. THURSDAY

O 6. FRIDAY

O 7. SATURDAY / 8. SUNDAY

IMPORTANT AS FUCK

SHIT TO DO

Notes and Shit

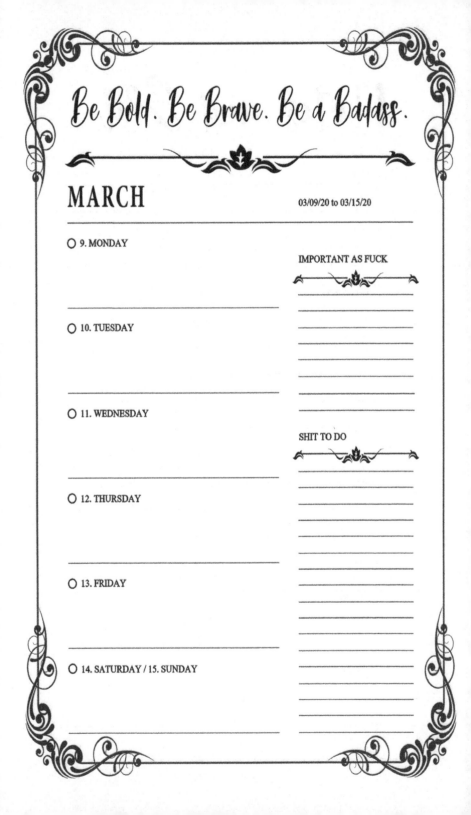

Be Bold. Be Brave. Be a Badass.

MARCH

03/09/20 to 03/15/20

O 9. MONDAY

IMPORTANT AS FUCK

O 10. TUESDAY

O 11. WEDNESDAY

SHIT TO DO

O 12. THURSDAY

O 13. FRIDAY

O 14. SATURDAY / 15. SUNDAY

Notes and Shit

JUST BE YOURSELF AND IF PEOPLE DON'T LIKE IT, FUCK THEM!

MARCH

03/16/20 to 03/22/20

O 16. MONDAY

IMPORTANT AS FUCK

O 17. TUESDAY

O 18. WEDNESDAY

SHIT TO DO

O 19. THURSDAY

O 20. FRIDAY

O 21. SATURDAY / 22. SUNDAY

Notes and Shit

YOU'RE DOING A BEAUTIFUL JOB AT FIGURING OUT SOME HEAVY SHIT

MARCH

03/23/20 to 03/29/20

O 23. MONDAY

O 24. TUESDAY

O 25. WEDNESDAY

O 26. THURSDAY

O 27. FRIDAY

O 28. SATURDAY / 29. SUNDAY

IMPORTANT AS FUCK

SHIT TO DO

Notes and Shit

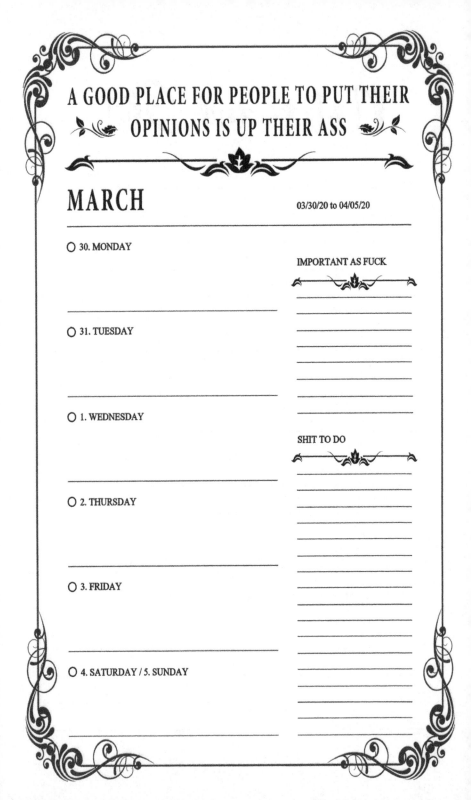

A GOOD PLACE FOR PEOPLE TO PUT THEIR OPINIONS IS UP THEIR ASS

MARCH

03/30/20 to 04/05/20

○ 30. MONDAY

IMPORTANT AS FUCK

○ 31. TUESDAY

○ 1. WEDNESDAY

SHIT TO DO

○ 2. THURSDAY

○ 3. FRIDAY

○ 4. SATURDAY / 5. SUNDAY

Notes and Shit

BE WHO YOU WERE BEFORE THE BULLSHIT DIMMED YOUR FUCKING SHINE

APRIL

04/06/20 to 04/12/20

○ 6. MONDAY

IMPORTANT AS FUCK

○ 7. TUESDAY

○ 8. WEDNESDAY

SHIT TO DO

○ 9. THURSDAY

○ 10. FRIDAY

○ 11. SATURDAY / 12. SUNDAY

Notes and Shit

you are fucking unstoppable

APRIL

04/13/20 to 04/19/20

○ 13. MONDAY

IMPORTANT AS FUCK

○ 14. TUESDAY

○ 15. WEDNESDAY

SHIT TO DO

○ 16. THURSDAY

○ 17. FRIDAY

○ 18. SATURDAY / 19. SUNDAY

Notes and Shit

YOU CAN HANDLE WHATEVER SHIT
THIS WEEK THROWS AT YOU

APRIL

04/20/20 to 04/26/20

○ 20. MONDAY

IMPORTANT AS FUCK

○ 21. TUESDAY

○ 22. WEDNESDAY

SHIT TO DO

○ 23. THURSDAY

○ 24. FRIDAY

○ 25. SATURDAY / 26. SUNDAY

Notes and Shit

Reminder: you are a badass

APRIL

04/27/20 to 05/03/20

○ 27. MONDAY

○ 28. TUESDAY

○ 29. WEDNESDAY

○ 30. THURSDAY

○ 1. FRIDAY

○ 2. SATURDAY / 3. SUNDAY

IMPORTANT AS FUCK

SHIT TO DO

Notes and Shit

IF YOU CAN DREAM IT, YOU CAN FUCKING DO IT

MAY

05/04/20 to 05/10/20

○ 4. MONDAY

○ 5. TUESDAY

○ 6. WEDNESDAY

○ 7. THURSDAY

○ 8. FRIDAY

○ 9. SATURDAY / 10. SUNDAY

IMPORTANT AS FUCK

SHIT TO DO

Notes and Shit

IT'S OKAY TO EXPERIENCE LIFE AT A RATE OF SEVERAL WTF'S PER HOUR

MAY

05/11/20 to 05/17/20

○ 11. MONDAY

IMPORTANT AS FUCK

○ 12. TUESDAY

○ 13. WEDNESDAY

SHIT TO DO

○ 14. THURSDAY

○ 15. FRIDAY

○ 16. SATURDAY / 17. SUNDAY

Notes and Shit

REMINDER: NO ONE HAS THEIR SHIT ALL TOGETHER

MAY

05/18/20 to 05/24/20

O 18. MONDAY

O 19. TUESDAY

O 20. WEDNESDAY

O 21. THURSDAY

O 22. FRIDAY

O 23. SATURDAY / 24. SUNDAY

IMPORTANT AS FUCK

SHIT TO DO

Notes and Shit

inhale the good shit. exhale the bullshit.

MAY

05/25/20 to 05/31/20

○ 25. MONDAY

IMPORTANT AS FUCK

○ 26. TUESDAY

○ 27. WEDNESDAY

SHIT TO DO

○ 28. THURSDAY

○ 29. FRIDAY

○ 30. SATURDAY / 31. SUNDAY

Notes and Shit

KEEP GOING, YOU HAVE A LOT OF MOTHERFUCKERS TO PROVE WRONG

JUNE

06/01/20 to 06/07/20

○ 1. MONDAY

IMPORTANT AS FUCK

○ 2. TUESDAY

○ 3. WEDNESDAY

SHIT TO DO

○ 4. THURSDAY

○ 5. FRIDAY

○ 6. SATURDAY / 7. SUNDAY

Notes and Shit

Make it fucking happen

JUNE

06/08/20 to 06/14/20

○ 8. MONDAY

IMPORTANT AS FUCK

○ 9. TUESDAY

○ 10. WEDNESDAY

SHIT TO DO

○ 11. THURSDAY

○ 12. FRIDAY

○ 13. SATURDAY / 14. SUNDAY

Notes and Shit

OTHER PEOPLE ARE EITHER ON YOUR SIDE, BY YOUR SIDE, OR IN YOUR FUCKING WAY

JUNE

06/15/20 to 06/21/20

○ 15. MONDAY

○ 16. TUESDAY

○ 17. WEDNESDAY

○ 18. THURSDAY

○ 19. FRIDAY

○ 20. SATURDAY / 21. SUNDAY

IMPORTANT AS FUCK

SHIT TO DO

Notes and Shit

save your fucks for magical shit

JUNE

06/22/20 to 06/28/20

O 22. MONDAY

IMPORTANT AS FUCK

O 23. TUESDAY

O 24. WEDNESDAY

SHIT TO DO

O 25. THURSDAY

O 26. FRIDAY

O 27. SATURDAY / 28. SUNDAY

Notes and Shit

BITCHILANTE: *noun*
A VIGILANTE BITCH WHO'S ONLY MEAN TO PEOPLE WHO DESERVE IT

JUNE

06/29/20 to 07/05/20

○ 29. MONDAY

○ 30. TUESDAY

○ 1. WEDNESDAY

○ 2. THURSDAY

○ 3. FRIDAY

○ 4. SATURDAY / 5. SUNDAY

IMPORTANT AS FUCK

SHIT TO DO

Notes and Shit

tell any negative thoughts to fuck off

JULY

07/06/20 to 07/12/20

O 6. MONDAY

IMPORTANT AS FUCK

O 7. TUESDAY

O 8. WEDNESDAY

SHIT TO DO

O 9. THURSDAY

O 10. FRIDAY

O 11. SATURDAY / 12. SUNDAY

Notes and Shit

FOLD YOUR WORRIES INTO PAPER PLANES AND TURN THEM INTO FLYING FUCKS

JULY

07/13/20 to 07/19/20

○ 13. MONDAY

IMPORTANT AS FUCK

○ 14. TUESDAY

○ 15. WEDNESDAY

SHIT TO DO

○ 16. THURSDAY

○ 17. FRIDAY

○ 18. SATURDAY / 19. SUNDAY

Notes and Shit

you are fucking beautiful

JULY

07/20/20 to 07/26/20

O 20. MONDAY

O 21. TUESDAY

O 22. WEDNESDAY

O 23. THURSDAY

O 24. FRIDAY

O 25. SATURDAY / 26. SUNDAY

IMPORTANT AS FUCK

SHIT TO DO

Notes and Shit

JUST A REMINDER THAT YOU DON'T HAVE TO PUT UP WITH ANYONE'S BULLSHIT

JULY

07/27/20 to 08/02/20

O 27. MONDAY

O 28. TUESDAY

O 29. WEDNESDAY

O 30. THURSDAY

O 31. FRIDAY

O 1. SATURDAY / 2. SUNDAY

IMPORTANT AS FUCK

SHIT TO DO

Notes and Shit

on the path to zero fucks and freedom

AUGUST

08/03/20 to 08/09/20

O 3. MONDAY

IMPORTANT AS FUCK

O 4. TUESDAY

O 5. WEDNESDAY

SHIT TO DO

O 6. THURSDAY

O 7. FRIDAY

O 8. SATURDAY / 9. SUNDAY

Notes and Shit

STOP DOUBTING YOURSELF,
YOU'RE A BADASS BITCH

AUGUST

08/10/20 to 08/16/20

○ 10. MONDAY

IMPORTANT AS FUCK

○ 11. TUESDAY

○ 12. WEDNESDAY

SHIT TO DO

○ 13. THURSDAY

○ 14. FRIDAY

○ 15. SATURDAY / 16. SUNDAY

Notes and Shit

WHEN LIFE GIVES YOU LEMONS, THROW THEM AT DOUCHEBAGS

AUGUST

08/17/20 to 08/23/20

○ 17. MONDAY

IMPORTANT AS FUCK

○ 18. TUESDAY

○ 19. WEDNESDAY

SHIT TO DO

○ 20. THURSDAY

○ 21. FRIDAY

○ 22. SATURDAY / 23. SUNDAY

Notes and Shit

TAKE A DEEP BREATH AND
FUCKING TRY AGAIN

AUGUST

08/24/20 to 08/30/20

○ 24. MONDAY

IMPORTANT AS FUCK

○ 25. TUESDAY

○ 26. WEDNESDAY

SHIT TO DO

○ 27. THURSDAY

○ 28. FRIDAY

○ 29. SATURDAY / 30. SUNDAY

Notes and Shit

do no harm but take no shit

SEPTEMBER

08/31/20 to 09/06/20

○ 31. MONDAY

○ 1. TUESDAY

○ 2. WEDNESDAY

○ 3. THURSDAY

○ 4. FRIDAY

○ 5. SATURDAY / 6. SUNDAY

IMPORTANT AS FUCK

SHIT TO DO

Notes and Shit

QUIT SLACKIN' AND MAKE THAT SHIT HAPPEN

SEPTEMBER

09/07/20 to 09/13/20

○ 7. MONDAY

○ 8. TUESDAY

○ 9. WEDNESDAY

○ 10. THURSDAY

○ 11. FRIDAY

○ 12. SATURDAY / 13. SUNDAY

IMPORTANT AS FUCK

SHIT TO DO

Notes and Shit

you are a kick ass warrior

SEPTEMBER

09/14/20 to 09/20/20

O 14. MONDAY

O 15. TUESDAY

O 16. WEDNESDAY

O 17. THURSDAY

O 18. FRIDAY

O 19. SATURDAY / 20. SUNDAY

IMPORTANT AS FUCK

SHIT TO DO

Notes and Shit

YOU DO NOT SPEW SWEAR WORDS, YOU ENUNCIATE THEM LIKE A FUCKING LADY

SEPTEMBER

09/21/20 to 09/27/20

O 21. MONDAY

O 22. TUESDAY

O 23. WEDNESDAY

O 24. THURSDAY

O 25. FRIDAY

O 26. SATURDAY / 27. SUNDAY

IMPORTANT AS FUCK

SHIT TO DO

Notes and Shit

ONLY GIVE A FUCK ABOUT THINGS
THAT SET YOUR SOUL ON FIRE

SEPTEMBER

09/28/20 to 10/04/20

O 28. MONDAY

IMPORTANT AS FUCK

O 29. TUESDAY

O 30. WEDNESDAY

SHIT TO DO

O 1. THURSDAY

O 2. FRIDAY

O 3. SATURDAY / 4. SUNDAY

Notes and Shit

you are a motherfucking legend

OCTOBER

10/05/20 to 10/11/20

○ 5. MONDAY

IMPORTANT AS FUCK

○ 6. TUESDAY

○ 7. WEDNESDAY

SHIT TO DO

○ 8. THURSDAY

○ 9. FRIDAY

○ 10. SATURDAY / 11. SUNDAY

Notes and Shit

DON'T LET STUPID SHIT STEAL YOUR HAPPINESS

OCTOBER

10/12/20 to 10/18/20

○ 12. MONDAY

○ 13. TUESDAY

○ 14. WEDNESDAY

○ 15. THURSDAY

○ 16. FRIDAY

○ 17. SATURDAY / 18. SUNDAY

IMPORTANT AS FUCK

SHIT TO DO

Notes and Shit

life is fucking tough but so are you

OCTOBER

10/19/20 to 10/25/20

O 19. MONDAY

IMPORTANT AS FUCK

O 20. TUESDAY

O 21. WEDNESDAY

SHIT TO DO

O 22. THURSDAY

O 23. FRIDAY

O 24. SATURDAY / 25. SUNDAY

Notes and Shit

YOU'RE THE BADDEST FUCKING
WITCH ON THE BLOCK

OCTOBER

10/26/20 to 11/01/20

O 26. MONDAY

O 27. TUESDAY

O 28. WEDNESDAY

O 29. THURSDAY

O 30. FRIDAY

O 31. SATURDAY / 1. SUNDAY

IMPORTANT AS FUCK

SHIT TO DO

Notes and Shit

DON'T QUIT. IF YOU'RE ALREADY IN PAIN, GET A FUCKING REWARD OUT OF IT

NOVEMBER

11/02/20 to 11/08/20

O 2. MONDAY

IMPORTANT AS FUCK

O 3. TUESDAY

O 4. WEDNESDAY

SHIT TO DO

O 5. THURSDAY

O 6. FRIDAY

O 7. SATURDAY / 8. SUNDAY

Notes and Shit

chin up, you fucking got this

NOVEMBER

11/09/20 to 11/15/20

O 9. MONDAY

IMPORTANT AS FUCK

O 10. TUESDAY

O 11. WEDNESDAY

SHIT TO DO

O 12. THURSDAY

O 13. FRIDAY

O 14. SATURDAY / 15. SUNDAY

Notes and Shit

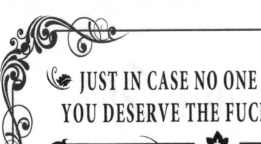

JUST IN CASE NO ONE TOLD YOU,
YOU DESERVE THE FUCKING WORLD

NOVEMBER

11/16/20 to 11/22/20

○ 16. MONDAY

IMPORTANT AS FUCK

○ 17. TUESDAY

○ 18. WEDNESDAY

SHIT TO DO

○ 19. THURSDAY

○ 20. FRIDAY

○ 21. SATURDAY / 22. SUNDAY

Notes and Shit

Show this clusterfuck who's boss

NOVEMBER

11/23/20 to 11/29/20

O 23. MONDAY

O 24. TUESDAY

O 25. WEDNESDAY

O 26. THURSDAY

O 27. FRIDAY

O 28. SATURDAY / 29. SUNDAY

IMPORTANT AS FUCK

SHIT TO DO

Notes and Shit

JUST SAY "FUCK IT" AND SPRINKLE
A LITTLE MAGIC ON IT

DECEMBER

11/30/20 to 12/06/20

O 30. MONDAY

IMPORTANT AS FUCK

O 1. TUESDAY

O 2. WEDNESDAY

SHIT TO DO

O 3. THURSDAY

O 4. FRIDAY

O 5. SATURDAY / 6. SUNDAY

Notes and Shit

every fucking thing is figureoutable

DECEMBER

12/07/20 to 12/13/20

O 7. MONDAY

IMPORTANT AS FUCK

O 8. TUESDAY

O 9. WEDNESDAY

SHIT TO DO

O 10. THURSDAY

O 11. FRIDAY

O 12. SATURDAY / 13. SUNDAY

Notes and Shit

DON'T GET HUNG UP ON SHIT
YOU CAN'T CONTROL

DECEMBER

12/14/20 to 12/20/20

O 14. MONDAY

IMPORTANT AS FUCK

O 15. TUESDAY

O 16. WEDNESDAY

SHIT TO DO

O 17. THURSDAY

O 18. FRIDAY

O 19. SATURDAY / 20. SUNDAY

Notes and Shit

MERRY EVERYTHING AND
HAPPY FUCKING ALWAYS

DECEMBER

12/21/20 to 12/27/20

○ 21. MONDAY

○ 22. TUESDAY

○ 23. WEDNESDAY

○ 24. THURSDAY

○ 25. FRIDAY

○ 26. SATURDAY / 27. SUNDAY

IMPORTANT AS FUCK

SHIT TO DO

Notes and Shit

CHEERS TO ANOTHER YEAR OF
BEING FUCKING FABULOUS

DECEMBER

12/28/20 to 01/03/21

O 28. MONDAY

O 29. TUESDAY

O 30. WEDNESDAY

O 31. THURSDAY

O 1. FRIDAY

O 2. SATURDAY / 3. SUNDAY

IMPORTANT AS FUCK

SHIT TO DO

Notes and Shit

January 2020

Sunday	Monday	Tuesday	Wednesday	Thursday	Friday	Saturday
29	30	31	1	2	3	4
5	6	7	8	9	10	11
12	13	14	15	16	17	18
19	20	21	22	23	24	25
26	27	28	29	30	31	1

Notes and Shit

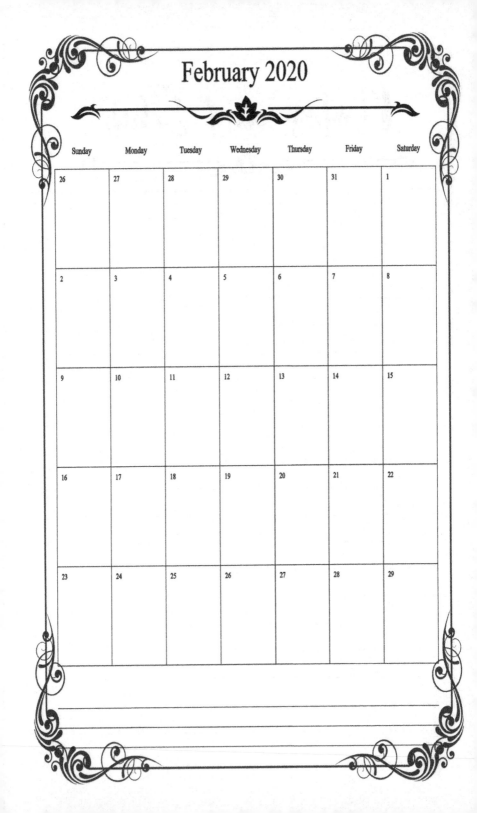

February 2020

Sunday	Monday	Tuesday	Wednesday	Thursday	Friday	Saturday
26	27	28	29	30	31	1
2	3	4	5	6	7	8
9	10	11	12	13	14	15
16	17	18	19	20	21	22
23	24	25	26	27	28	29

Notes and Shit

March 2020

Sunday	Monday	Tuesday	Wednesday	Thursday	Friday	Saturday
1	2	3	4	5	6	7
8	9	10	11	12	13	14
15	16	17	18	19	20	21
22	23	24	25	26	27	28
29	30	31	1	2	3	4

Notes and Shit

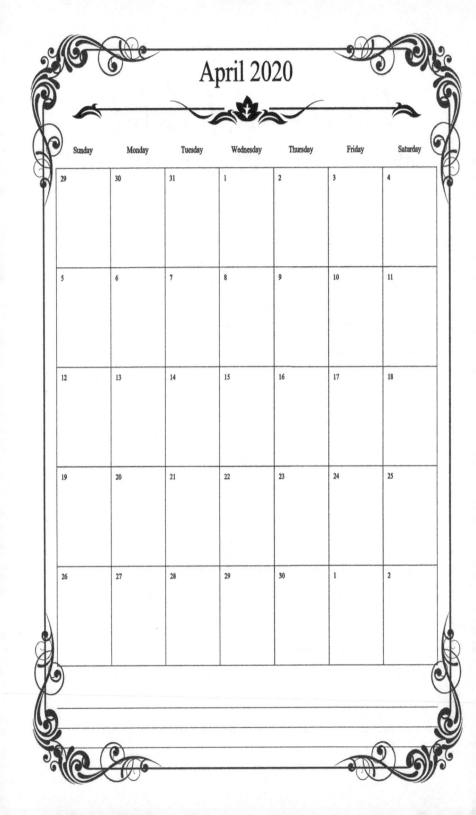

April 2020

Sunday	Monday	Tuesday	Wednesday	Thursday	Friday	Saturday
29	30	31	1	2	3	4
5	6	7	8	9	10	11
12	13	14	15	16	17	18
19	20	21	22	23	24	25
26	27	28	29	30	1	2

Notes and Shit

May 2020

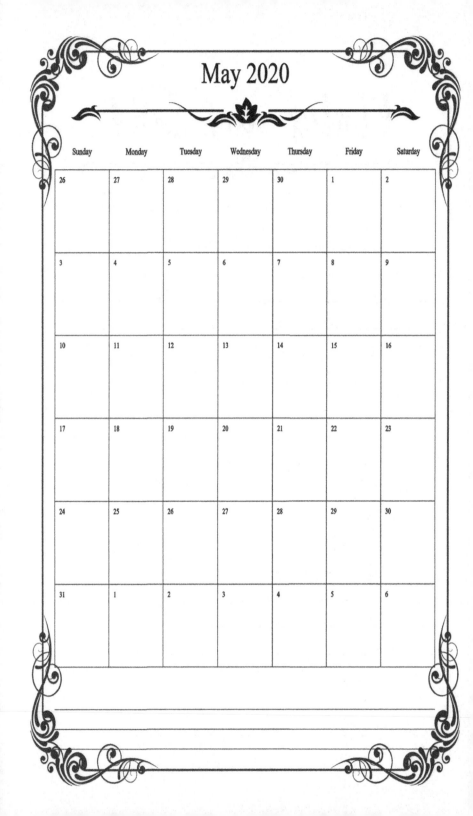

Sunday	Monday	Tuesday	Wednesday	Thursday	Friday	Saturday
26	27	28	29	30	1	2
3	4	5	6	7	8	9
10	11	12	13	14	15	16
17	18	19	20	21	22	23
24	25	26	27	28	29	30
31	1	2	3	4	5	6

Notes and Shit

June 2020

Sunday	Monday	Tuesday	Wednesday	Thursday	Friday	Saturday
31	1	2	3	4	5	6
7	8	9	10	11	12	13
14	15	16	17	18	19	20
21	22	23	24	25	26	27
28	29	30	1	2	3	4

Notes and Shit

July 2020

Sunday	Monday	Tuesday	Wednesday	Thursday	Friday	Saturday
28	29	30	1	2	3	4
5	6	7	8	9	10	11
12	13	14	15	16	17	18
19	20	21	22	23	24	25
26	27	28	29	30	31	1

Notes and Shit

August 2020

Sunday	Monday	Tuesday	Wednesday	Thursday	Friday	Saturday
26	27	28	29	30	31	1
2	3	4	5	6	7	8
9	10	11	12	13	14	15
16	17	18	19	20	21	22
23	24	25	26	27	28	29
30	31	1	2	3	4	5

Notes and Shit

September 2020

Sunday	Monday	Tuesday	Wednesday	Thursday	Friday	Saturday
30	31	1	2	3	4	5
6	7	8	9	10	11	12
13	14	15	16	17	18	19
20	21	22	23	24	25	26
27	28	29	30	1	2	3

Notes and Shit

October 2020

Sunday	Monday	Tuesday	Wednesday	Thursday	Friday	Saturday
27	28	29	30	1	2	3
4	5	6	7	8	9	10
11	12	13	14	15	16	17
18	19	20	21	22	23	24
25	26	27	28	29	30	31

Notes and Shit

November 2020

Sunday	Monday	Tuesday	Wednesday	Thursday	Friday	Saturday
1	2	3	4	5	6	7
8	9	10	11	12	13	14
15	16	17	18	19	20	21
22	23	24	25	26	27	28
29	30	1	2	3	4	5

Notes and Shit

December 2020

Sunday	Monday	Tuesday	Wednesday	Thursday	Friday	Saturday
29	30	1	2	3	4	5
6	7	8	9	10	11	12
13	14	15	16	17	18	19
20	21	22	23	24	25	26
27	28	29	30	31	1	2

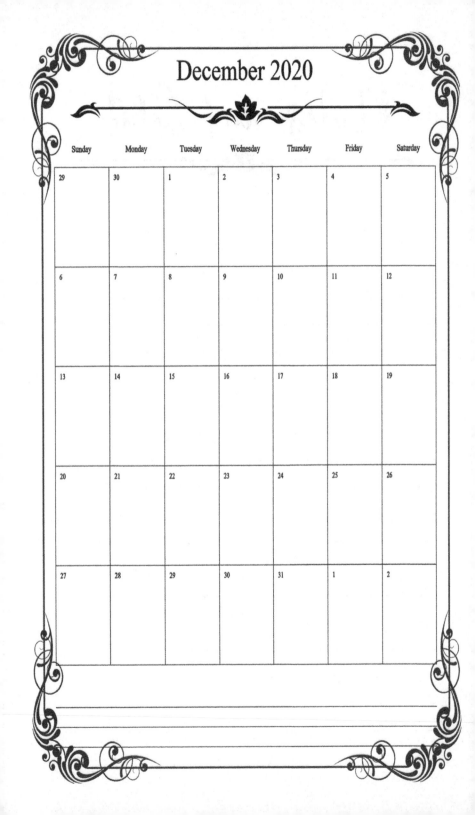

Notes and Shit

Made in the USA
Middletown, DE
08 May 2020